The Man Who Never Died

Fr. Gerald T. Brennan

The Man
Who Never Died

The Life and Adventures
of St. Peter, the First Pope

SOPHIA INSTITUTE PRESS®
Manchester, New Hampshire

The Man Who Never Died was originally published in 1946 by the Bruce Publishing Company, Milwaukee. This 2005 edition by Sophia Institute Press® includes minor editorial revisions and new illustrations.

Copyright © 2005 Sophia Institute Press®

Printed in the United States of America

Illustrations and cover design by Theodore Schluenderfritz

Sophia Institute Press®
Box 5284, Manchester, NH 03108
1-800-888-9344
www.sophiainstitute.com

Nihil obstat: William F. Bergan
Imprimatur: James E. Kearney,
Bishop of Rochester
August 13, 1945

Library of Congress Cataloging-in-Publication Data

Brennan, Gerald T., 1898-1962.
The man who never died : the life and adventures of St. Peter, the first pope / Gerald T. Brennan.
    p. cm.
ISBN 1-933184-09-4 (pbk. : alk. paper)
1. Peter, the Apostle, Saint. 2. Jesus Christ — Biography — Juvenile literature. I. Title.

BS2515.B733 2005
225.9'2 — dc22
                                              2005018046

*To a little friend of mine, John Gerrit,
with the hope that he and others
may learn to love the Faith
from The Man Who Never Died*

Contents

The Man Who Never Died

Chapter 1

The Fisherman in the Desert

A desert was a strange place for a fisherman. But Simon, the fisherman, was doing some strange fishing.

Simon had spent most of his twenty-nine years on the Lake of Galilee. All his life he had been a fisherman — a fisherman on the Lake of Galilee.

As a boy, Simon often sat in his father's boat and listened to his stories. "God has promised us a Redeemer," his father would say, "and someday the Redeemer will walk this earth. The Redeemer will be a great King. A mighty King who will rule the whole world!"

Time and time again, young Simon asked his father questions. "When will the Redeemer come? Where will He live? What will be His name?" But his father could not answer those questions. No one knew when the Redeemer would come. No one knew where He would live. No one knew what His name would be.

For hundreds of years the world had waited for the Redeemer, and the world was still waiting. Millions of men lived and died, and they did not see the Redeemer. Simon's father lived and died, and he never saw the

Redeemer. But young Simon did not lose hope. He knew that someday the Redeemer would come. Someday God would keep His promise.

The years passed quickly for Simon the fisherman. They were not exciting years, but years of simple living. Simon loved his home; he loved the lake. He liked the peace and quiet of his little town of Bethsaida.

But one day there was great excitement in Bethsaida. A traveler brought word that a man called John the Baptist was preaching in the desert of Judea.

"This John," said the traveler, "wears a garment of camel hair with a skin about his waist. He eats nothing except birds and honey. He says that the Redeemer will soon be here."

At first people would not believe. But later they heard more stories about John the Baptist. Then people began to wonder if John had been sent by God. They wondered, too, if John was the Redeemer.

People from all over Galilee hurried down to Judea. Simon, too, left his boat and his nets, and his brother Andrew went with him.

While in Judea, the brothers lived in a small cabin near

the Jordan River, and each day they went into the desert to hear John the Baptist.

"Do penance!" was John's message. "The Redeemer will soon be here."

"The Redeemer will soon be here!" That was very good news for Simon and Andrew. Each day the brothers waited, and each day they prayed — prayed that they would see the Redeemer and that they would not be disappointed.

Then Andrew went to the desert alone one day. He was gone all day, and when evening came, he did not return. Simon began to worry. He was afraid something might have happened to his brother. He walked back and forth in front of the cabin, his rough hands held tightly behind his back. Now and then he stopped to listen, but all was quiet. There were no footsteps, no Andrew.

After some time, Simon thought that he had heard a noise. He did hear a noise. Someone was coming.

"Is that you, Andrew?" called Simon.

"Yes!" came the answer through the darkness. "I have good news!"

Simon was excited. "What is it?" he asked. But Simon had to wait until Andrew reached the cabin. "I have seen the Redeemer, and I have talked with Him. We have been together since four o'clock."

Simon could hardly believe the words. His brother had seen the Redeemer! At last, the Redeemer had come.

Andrew tried to answer his brother's questions.

He told how John the Baptist had shown him the Redeemer, how he had followed the Redeemer to His cabin by the river. He tried to remember everything, every word that the Redeemer had spoken. The thing that surprised Simon most was to hear that the Redeemer was a Man from Nazareth. A Man about thirty years of age! A Man who was not a king! A Man who called Himself Jesus.

The more Simon heard, the more impatient he became. Finally, he begged his brother to take him to Jesus. Andrew led the way, and the two men hurried through the darkness. They walked some distance before they came to a cabin, the door of which was open. Near the door sat a Man — alone. The Man was Jesus.

Jesus arose, walked toward the brothers, and placed His hand upon Simon's shoulder. "You are Simon, the son of Jona," He said. "You shall be called Peter."

Simon was so surprised that he couldn't speak.

The Redeemer knew him, called him by name, and changed his name to Peter. It was hard for Simon to understand.

For a long time Jesus talked with the two men.

When the visit was over, Andrew and Simon went back to their cabin. There were two happy brothers in Judea that night. But Simon Peter was especially happy. He had gone into the desert to fish. He had caught his fish. Simon Peter had met Jesus Christ.

Chapter 2

Peter Goes to a Wedding

Peter and Andrew walked along a lonely country road. They were going home. But the brothers were not alone. Jesus was with them. When Jesus heard that Peter and Andrew were going back to Galilee, He decided to go with them. He had been away for three months, and He was eager to see His Mother.

For three days, the men had traveled through Judea, Samaria, and Galilee. As they drew near the village of Cana in Galilee, Jesus surprised His companions.

"I am going to a wedding at Cana," He said, "and I want you to come with me. My Mother will be there, and I want you to meet her."

Mary, the Mother of Jesus, would be at the wedding. Mary, the wife of Joseph, the carpenter! Surely Peter and Andrew could not refuse this invitation.

"Master," said Peter, "You are very kind. It will be an honor for us to meet Your Mother."

When the men reached Cana, they went to the home of Nathaniel. The wedding was over, but the house was still crowded with relatives and friends. Some of them

7

were dancing; others were feasting. Everyone seemed to be very happy.

At first, Peter did not have a good time because it was hard for him to meet strangers. But he found the Mother of Jesus very kind and friendly. Her quiet, simple manner won Peter's heart and made him feel as though he had known her for a long time. At times, Mary seemed very serious, and there was something sad about her smile. But she was good company — an interesting talker, a good listener.

Jesus, Mary, and their companions stood near the place where the servants were gathered together. After a little while, Peter heard some of the servants grumble. Something was wrong. Peter turned his head and tried to listen.

"There is not enough wine," he heard the servants say. "The wine will soon be gone. What shall we do?"

Peter was not the only one who heard the servants. Mary, too, heard them say the wine would soon be gone. At once, the Mother of Jesus began to worry. She knew that the bride and groom would feel very bad if there was not enough wine. The servants would be blamed for it, and the crowd would be disappointed. Something had to be done, and it had to be done quickly.

Mary turned to Jesus. "Son," she said as she pointed to the servants, "they have no wine."

Peter wondered why Mary had spoken to Jesus. Did Mary think that Jesus could help?

Mary left her companions and walked over to the servants to talk to them. In a few moments, Jesus was close by her side.

Now, there were six large stone jugs, or waterpots, on the ground. The waterpots were empty.

"Fill those jugs with water," said Jesus to the servants.

One of the servants laughed. "Water?" he said aloud. "Water at a wedding? Who ever heard of serving water at a wedding?"

Jesus paid no attention to the servant's questions.

He watched the other servants draw water from a well. Then the water was carried and emptied into the jugs.

When the six waterpots were filled, Jesus raised His hand and looked toward Heaven. He did not speak.

"What is He going to do?" Peter asked himself.

"Now, empty the waterpots," Jesus said.

The servants obeyed and emptied the first waterpot. And what a surprise! The servants did not pour water. They poured wine.

Peter could hardly believe his eyes. He had seen a miracle. Christ's first miracle! Peter had seen Jesus change water into wine.

Chapter 3

The Brothers Receive an Invitation

Peter and Andrew went back home to Bethsaida on the shore of the Lake of Galilee. They had met the Redeemer. They had talked with Him. They had seen Him perform a miracle. No wonder they were happy!

Months passed. A whole year passed. During all that time, Peter did not see Christ. But Peter did not forget. Oh, no! Many, many times Peter thought about Christ, and about what He had said, and about the miracle He had done. Peter longed for the day when he would see the Redeemer again.

Night after night, Peter and Andrew fished on the Lake of Galilee. Fishing was always better at night, and as they worked, the brothers often spoke about Christ. They wondered when they would see the Redeemer again. They wondered where He was and what He was doing.

In the morning, when their fishing was done, the brothers sat on the shore, mending and cleaning their nets. As they worked, they talked about many things. But most of the time their talk was about the Redeemer.

Then, one day, Peter heard good news. A man told him that Jesus was in the nearby town of Capharnaum. He had been there for some time. Not only was Jesus in Capharnaum, but He was preaching there. He was teaching the people about God.

This was the best news that Peter had heard in a long time. Why, it was only a short distance to Capharnaum. Right then and there, Peter decided that he would go to Capharnaum.

He hurried into the house to tell his brother.

"Andrew," he called as he opened the door, "Jesus is in Capharnaum. We must go there next Saturday."

Andrew was excited, and he agreed to go with his brother. They planned to leave early on Saturday morning. They wanted to meet Jesus and hear Him preach.

Men often make plans, but God changes them.

Little did Peter and Andrew think that God would change their plans. But that is what happened.

That evening, Peter and Andrew went fishing, as they had done so many times in the past. They fished all night, and the time passed quickly. The fishing was good, and both men were in fine spirits. Neither one knew the other's thoughts, but both were thinking about the same thing: the coming Saturday — the day when the fishermen would see Christ!

Morning came, and with it came a surprise. As the brothers drew near the shore, they saw a Man. The Man was watching them, and He seemed to be waiting for them. They had seen that Man before. Was it . . . ? Yes, it was! The Man was Jesus.

Peter raised his hand, and Andrew nodded his head. Then both men pulled in their net. The brothers were excited, and many thoughts ran through their minds. They wondered what Jesus was doing in Bethsaida. Why had He come? What did He want?

When the net was placed in the bottom of the boat, the brothers raised their heads. They looked at Christ, and He looked at them.

Then the soft voice of Christ rolled across the water. "My friends," He said, "come, follow me, and I will make you fishers of men."

Fishers of men!

Christ called the brothers to be fishers of men. Christ asked them to be His disciples. He wanted Peter and Andrew to leave their home, their fishing, and the lake they loved. He wanted them to teach and catch men.

Peter was the first to leave the boat. He waded through the water and was soon on shore. Andrew was close behind.

For some time Jesus talked to the brothers. He told them many interesting things, and Peter and Andrew listened to every word. It was good to be with Jesus again.

As the three left the shore, Peter turned for one last look. During the days that followed, Peter spent little time fishing on the Lake of Galilee. He did a different kind of fishing. Peter caught men.

Chapter 4

Christ Shows His Power

It was Saturday in Capharnaum — that pleasant little town that rested beside the Lake of Galilee. And Saturday was the day of prayer! The day when all good Jews went to church.

Rich and poor left their homes that morning and made their way to the center of the town. There, in all its glory, stood the church, a beautiful building — in fact, one of the most beautiful buildings in Galilee. Those simple people loved their church. They were proud of their church. It was the center of their religious life.

Jesus, too, went to church that morning, and Peter went with Him. For an hour they prayed together. Prayed with the others. Prayed that God would bless them, and thanked God for His graces.

When the prayers were finished, Jesus spoke to the crowd. "Do penance!" He urged them again and again. "You must do penance if you wish to go to Heaven."

It was easy for the people to understand Christ. He spoke clearly, used simple words, and told interesting stories. He was honest, sincere, and spoke with power.

When the service was over, Jesus left the church.

Peter and three companions followed Him. The five men turned to the left, walked down a narrow street, and were soon at the home of Peter's mother-in-law. They went there for their morning meal.

But something was wrong. Everyone in the house was excited. Peter's mother-in-law was sick, very sick with a fever. Peter hurried into the bedroom, and lying on a bed was his wife's mother. Her eyes stared at the low ceiling. Her cheeks and lips were burning, and her hands were very warm.

Peter asked no questions. He knew his mother-in-law would not live long. Her time would soon be over. She would be gone. Peter looked at the woman and shook his head.

For a moment, he forgot that Jesus was in the next room. But just then the door opened, and Jesus entered the bedroom.

"The woman is dying," said Peter to Christ. "She is burning with fever."

Jesus acted as though He did not hear, and He paid no attention to Peter. Jesus looked at the sick woman and held her hand. Then

He ordered the fever to leave her. In a few moments, the woman sat up in bed. The fever was gone. The woman was cured.

Then Jesus and Peter turned and left the room.

Peter tried to thank Christ, but words were not necessary. Jesus understood.

In a short time, the morning meal was ready.

Jesus and His four companions sat at a table in the center of the room. A door opened, and a woman brought in some food. The woman was Peter's mother-in-law.

Once again, Peter had seen a miracle. He had seen a sick woman made well. Once again, Peter had seen the power of Christ. It was not the power of a man. It was the power of God.

Chapter 5

The Call

Peter was not a rich man. He had made a fair living at fishing, but that was all. Now that he was with the Redeemer, he still had to make a living. So he left Christ for a few days and went back to Bethsaida.

One morning Peter and Andrew returned from one of their trips. They had fished all night, and they had caught nothing. Both men were so disappointed that they did not feel like talking. Suddenly, Peter happened to look toward the shore.

"Look at the crowd of people!" said Peter excitedly. "I wonder what's the matter."

As the fishermen drew near shore, they learned why the people were there. They had followed Jesus to the lake and were crowding about Him. They wanted to hear Jesus speak.

When Peter and Andrew reached the shore, Jesus stepped into the boat and asked Peter to row out into the lake. Peter was only too happy to help his Friend. He rowed a little way from the shore and anchored the boat. Then Jesus turned and spoke to the people. While He talked, Peter sat at His feet. Every word that was spoken sank deep into Peter's heart.

When Jesus finished, the crowd was silent. Jesus had spoken powerful words, and the people were thinking. They wondered, too, whether Jesus would come on shore. They wanted to tell Him how much they enjoyed His words.

But Jesus did not go on shore. He turned to Peter and gave a command.

"Row out where the water is deep," ordered Christ, "and let down your nets for a catch!"

Peter's dark eyes flashed with surprise, as he rubbed his thick hair with his rough hand.

"Master," he replied, "we have fished all night and have caught nothing. But at Your word I will let down the net."

The brothers knew that the best fish were caught at night. Now the sun was shining brightly. To fish in the sunshine was only a waste of time. But Peter and Andrew obeyed Christ and rowed out into deep water. They dropped their net so that it would drag along after them. Suddenly, the boat stopped. The men tried to row ahead, but the boat would not move. Something was holding them back. Perhaps the net was caught. Oh, but the net was not caught. The net was full of fish!

Fish! Hundreds of shining fish! Never before had Peter seen so many fish in his net. In his excitement, he tugged and pulled the net, and he called to Andrew to

help him. They pulled together, but the load was too heavy. The net broke.

It was a terrible time for the net to break, but two friends, standing on the shore, saw that the brothers were in trouble. The friends hurried into a boat and were soon by the side of Peter and Andrew. The four men pulled the net carefully and filled both boats with the shining fish.

During all this excitement, Jesus sat in Peter's boat. He did not speak, nor did He offer to help. He smiled at the men and was very calm.

Peter had forgotten about Jesus. He had forgotten that Jesus was in the boat. But when he turned and saw Christ, everything was clear to him. Now he knew how he had caught so many fish. Jesus had brought the fish to his net. Again, Jesus had shown His power. He had performed a miracle — another miracle in Peter's boat.

Peter's heart beat quickly. But somehow, he did not know what to say. He fell on his knees and looked up into the face of Christ.

Jesus knew what was in Peter's heart. He knew that Peter was grateful. Placing His hand on Peter's shoulder, He spoke softly. "Henceforth you shall catch men."

That was a strange morning on the Lake of Galilee. The fishermen caught fish, but Christ caught the fishermen — Peter and Andrew.

Chapter 6

The Twelve

It was night. Midnight. The world was asleep, and the town of Capharnaum was quiet. But there was one Man from Capharnaum who was not at rest. That Man was Jesus.

The Redeemer was on the top of a nearby mountain — alone. He had gone to the mountain to pray. The next morning, Jesus would have to make an important decision. He was going to take one of the most important steps of His whole life. He prayed to God to help Him. He begged His Father to guide Him. That was Christ's prayer through that long, dark night.

Morning came, and Jesus walked down from the mountain. As usual, there was a crowd of people waiting for Him. Of course, Jesus was pleased. He raised His hand, and the crowd became silent. For several minutes, the people waited for Christ to speak.

But that morning, Jesus did not teach.

He looked at all the faces before Him, hundreds of them, and then He called twelve names: "Peter! Andrew! James, the son of Zebedee! John! Philip! Bartholomew!

Matthew! Thomas! James, the son of Alpheus! Simon! Jude! Judas!"

Each name was spoken slowly and clearly. As each name was called, the man who answered to that name left the crowd and walked toward Christ. Then Jesus led the twelve away.

"I have chosen you to be my Apostles," said Christ to the twelve men. "You will stay with me and be my helpers, and soon you will take my place. You will teach and preach. You will heal the sick."

Christ chose those twelve men to be His Apostles.

Twelve special friends who lived with Christ, worked with Him, helped Him. Twelve men with simple hearts, but those hearts were filled with love for Christ. Those men left their homes, friends, everything, and followed the Redeemer. They were the twelve Apostles of Jesus Christ!

Jesus had told Peter that He would make him a fisher of men. Peter was now an Apostle. He was one of the chosen twelve. Jesus had kept His promise.

Chapter 7

Peter Learns a Great Truth

For three years, Christ and Peter were close friends. They were partners in everything. And those three years were very happy ones for Peter. They were years when the apostle learned to know Christ, and to know Christ was to love Him. They were years when secrets were told and plans were made. They were years in which Peter saw and heard many strange things.

There was the day when Peter saw Christ bring a dead man back to life. The day when Christ gave sight to a blind man. The day when Jesus cured the lame and the deaf. Those were things that no man could do, and yet they were done by Christ.

And what did Peter think of those strange things?

At first, Peter was surprised, and then he wondered: "Where does Jesus get His great power? How can Christ do these things? Those questions puzzled the apostle.

Before many weeks had passed, Peter had the answer to those questions. Christ was performing miracles; He was doing things that no other man could do. Jesus had power over the sick and the dead. Why, that power belonged only to God. Yes, that was the answer. Jesus was a Man, and He was more than a man. Jesus was God.

The thought that Jesus was God sank deep into Peter's heart, and it filled him with zeal. He knew that he was God's partner and that he was living with God, working with God, helping God.

Every day with Christ was a day of excitement, but there was one day, in particular, that Peter never forgot. It was the day Christ and His Apostles went into the desert. They wanted to be alone, but five thousand people followed them. Jesus, however, was kind to the people. In fact, He performed a miracle for them. Jesus fed those five thousand people with five loaves of bread and two fishes.

To Peter, that was one of Christ's greatest miracles. It was a new kind of miracle, and that miracle was enough. Peter did not need any more proof. He was certain now that Christ was God.

That night Peter was to learn again.

After Jesus had fed the five thousand in the desert, He ordered the Apostles to go home. They had gone into the desert with Christ, and now He was sending them away.

The Apostles left Christ, walked down to the shore, and entered their boat. They had little to say, but each one wondered: Why doesn't Christ come with us? Why is He remaining behind?

That night it was dark and cold on the Lake of Galilee. There was a strong wind, and Peter and his friends found it hard to manage the boat. After a while, the wind became stronger and the waves rose higher. The men tried to steer and guide their boat, but the wind and waves tossed it about this way and that. The men were in danger, and they knew it. Any moment the boat might sink. They were afraid, terribly afraid that they would drown and every moment would be their last.

Suddenly, a light appeared on the water. A bright light! A very strong light! And the light moved toward the boat. Twelve hearts pounded with fear, and twelve voices cried out in terror.

But then the light seemed to change. The light *did* change. It changed into the figure of a Man. And the Man was walking toward them — *on the water.*

"Take courage. It is I. Do not be afraid," came a voice across the water.

That voice! The Apostles had heard it before.

The voice of Jesus! The voice of the Master!

Peter was the first to answer. "Lord," he called, "if it is You, let me come to You over the water."

Christ's answer was one word: "Come!"

That was enough for Peter. In an instant the apostle was on his feet. He stepped out of the boat, stood on the water, and walked toward Christ. It all happened so quickly that Peter didn't realize what he was doing. As he drew near Christ, Peter lost faith and began to worry. He wondered whether the water would hold him. And at once he began to sink.

"Lord, save me!" cried Peter at the top of his voice.

But Jesus was near. He caught Peter by the hand and raised him up. And together, Christ and Peter walked hand in hand upon the water. In a short time they were in the boat with the other eleven apostles.

Then the sea became calm. The Apostles were no longer afraid. Christ had come to them. He was with them. Now there was no danger.

Hand in hand, Christ and Peter walked upon the water. And together they walked down through the years.

Chapter 8

The Leader

During the month that followed, Jesus preached, taught, and performed miracles. Yet many people refused to believe in Him. Some wanted proof from Heaven that He was the Redeemer. Others found fault with His miracles. Still others would not listen. Many followed Him for a time, then left Him. There were some who even hated Christ — hated His words, hated His miracles. No matter what He did, many refused to believe that He was the Son of God.

Those people had been taught that the Redeemer would be a great King. But they found that Christ was not a king. He had no land, no riches, and no servants. He was a poor Man from Galilee, the Son of a carpenter. Those people knew that Christ did great things, but they would not accept Him as the Redeemer. Christ, they said, was a great Man, but they refused to say that He was God.

Those people disturbed Christ. After all, He had come to save all men. He wanted all men to follow Him. He wanted all men to be saved.

During that month of disappointment, Christ spent much time in prayer. He prayed for His enemies and for those who would not believe in Him. He prayed that His Father would soften their hearts, that they would have faith, that they would believe.

While many did not believe in Christ, we must remember that thousands of others did believe in Him. Wherever He went, people crowded about Him. They listened to His words and believed what He taught. Those faithful ones were Christ's greatest encouragement, His great happiness. But Christ wanted *all* men. He wanted no enemies. He wanted all men to follow Him.

Finally, one day, Jesus decided to test His Apostles. Did the Apostles believe in Him? Did they believe that He was the Redeemer? Did the Apostles have any doubts? He decided to find out what were their thoughts.

"Who do men say that I am?" Jesus asked them.

There were many answers to that question. The Apostles told Christ that some people thought He was John the Baptist. Others thought that He was Elijah. Some thought that He was Jeremiah, or one of the prophets.

Jesus listened to the answers. He was disappointed. Then Christ asked another question.

"But who do you say that I am?"

Some of the Apostles turned and looked at one another. But Peter was not lost for an answer. Without waiting a moment, the apostle said, "Thou art the Christ, the Son of the living God."

That answer made Christ smile. He was pleased.

Peter had spoken for the Twelve, and he had spoken well. Jesus knew that His Apostles believed.

Jesus stared at Peter for some time. He smiled again and then spoke to the apostle: "Thou art Peter, and upon this rock I will build my Church."

The Apostles were silent. Never before had Christ spoken such words.

But Peter! It was a solemn moment for Peter. His heart beat quickly, because he knew the meaning of those words. Christ had called him a rock, and Christ planned to build His Church upon him. Christ had chosen Peter to be a leader. The leader of the Apostles! The head of His Church!

"Thou art Peter, and upon this rock I will build my Church." With those words, Christ founded His Church. Today, hundreds of years after the death of Christ, that Church still stands. And the Church of Christ will stand until the end of time, because it is built upon a rock.

Chapter 9

Christ Prepares His Apostles

P eter was now the Rock. He was the leader of the
Apostles, the head of Christ's Church. He was the
favorite one of the Twelve.

You might think that that honor made a change in
Peter. You might think that it made him proud. But that
is not true. Instead, Peter was always kind and very humble. In fact, he was one of the most humble of the Apostles. Always anxious to learn, ever ready to help, he tried
more than ever to please his Master. With him Christ
was always first — first in his obedience, first in his de-
votion, first in his love. Peter was determined to be loyal
to Christ because he wanted to thank Christ for the faith
and trust that had been placed in him.

The other apostles looked upon Peter as their leader,
their guide. Not one of them was jealous of him. They
knew that Peter was their friend, and they were loyal to
him. They trusted him, and they loved him.

Thus, Jesus had made no mistakes. He made no mistake in the men whom He had chosen as Apostles. He
made no mistake in naming Peter as the leader of His

little group. The Apostles had one desire, one ambition: to lead the whole world to the feet of Christ. They preached, taught, and helped men save their souls.

Once the Apostles had been strangers to one another, but now they were friends. Brothers! Christ's Helpers! Apostles!

The days with Christ were happy days for the Apostles. During all those months, they were never sorry for having followed Him. They always found their Master kind, helpful, cheerful, and pleasant.

But then there came a change, and Peter was the first to see it. The apostle noticed that Jesus spent a great deal of time alone. He wondered why Jesus spent so much time in prayer. Was He worried or afraid? Did He know something that He was not telling the Apostles? For several days, Jesus seemed very sad and He seldom smiled. There was something on the Master's mind. Something was wrong, and Peter knew it.

Peter said nothing to the other apostles. He asked no questions, and he kept his fears to himself.

Then, one day, Peter heard a strange story. There were Jews in Jerusalem who hated Christ and wanted to kill Him. And why? Because Jesus had cured a crippled boy on the Sabbath day. The Sabbath, you know, was the day of rest. Christ had worked a miracle on the Sabbath. He had worked a miracle on the holy day of the Jews.

There were Jews who wanted to kill Christ! After all the kind things Jesus had done, how could anyone want to kill Him? Peter could hardly believe the story. He was greatly disturbed. He was worried. Afraid!

At first Peter decided that he would tell his brother Andrew. But then Peter changed his mind. He did not tell Andrew, nor did he tell the other apostles. He did not want the apostles to worry or ask questions. Perhaps the story was not true!

But the story was true, and Jesus knew it. That was the reason Jesus kept away from the city of Jerusalem. That was why Jesus was sad. He knew only too well that there were dark days ahead. There would soon be trouble.

Little by little Jesus began to prepare His Apostles. He began to talk about death — His death. At first the Apostles were disturbed. They wondered why Jesus talked about dying. After all, He was a young Man. He was strong and in good health. The Apostles felt that He would live for a long time.

Christ knew that the Apostles did not understand. So, one day in Galilee, He told them everything. "The Son of Man," He said, "is to be betrayed into the hands of men, and they will kill Him. And having been killed, He will rise again on the third day."

Those words shocked the twelve Apostles. The Master will be betrayed! He will be handed over to His enemies! Men will kill Jesus! They will put Him to death! And after three days, Jesus will rise again!

Those were terrible words, and they were hard to believe.

The Man Who Never Died

Many times Peter thought about those words of Christ. Men will put Christ to death! Will Christ's death mean the end of everything? What will happen to the twelve Apostles? Peter wondered.

Chapter 10

The Fall

The months passed quickly. Six months in all! Jesus spent those months in the towns and villages outside the city of Jerusalem. He preached very often, but He did not perform many miracles. During that time, His enemies tried hard to trap Him, but they could not catch Him with their questions.

Jesus tried to win His enemies. He wanted their hearts. He wanted, especially, the hearts of the people of Jerusalem. Twice He even dared to go into that city, and He preached and taught there. But the hearts of the people were hard. They listened to Christ, but they refused to believe in Him.

Those six months were bitter months for the leader of the Apostles. Peter was not a coward, but He worried about Christ. He knew that Christ was in danger. He knew that some men wanted to kill the Master.

Peter always felt better when Jesus was away from Jerusalem. There was less danger then, because Christ was away from His enemies. But Jesus decided to celebrate the feast of the Pasch in Jerusalem. The Pasch, you know, was the great feast day of the Jews. It was a day when no one worked. It was a day of feasting.

Jesus was going to celebrate the Pasch in Jerusalem! That was bad news for Peter. Again the apostle began to worry. He felt that Christ was taking too many chances. Jesus was placing Himself in danger. But Peter did not try to keep his Master from going.

Jesus and His Apostles celebrated the Pasch in the city of Jerusalem. At that supper, Jesus worked one of His greatest miracles. He changed bread and wine into His Body and Blood, and He gave His Body and Blood to the Apostles to eat and drink. Thus, the Apostles were the first ones to receive Holy Communion. Then Christ did something more. He gave the Apostles the power to change bread and wine into His Body and Blood. He made the Apostles priests. His first priests! The first priests of the Catholic Church!

Peter was happy. He had received the Body and Blood of Christ. He was now a priest. How could he ever thank Christ for all that He had done? Peter knew that there was only one way to thank Christ, and that was to be a good priest, the best priest of the Twelve.

Before they left the table, Jesus became very sad.

"One of you," He said, "will betray me, and when my enemies come, the rest of you will run away and deny me."

Those words were too much for the apostle Peter. "The others may run away and deny You, but I will never deny You," said Peter strongly, and he meant every word.

Jesus waited a moment. Then He turned to Peter and warned him. "Amen, I say to you, this very night, you will deny me."

Peter did not agree with his Master. Deep down in his heart, he felt that Jesus was wrong. He would never deny Christ. Never!

It was late now. It was time to go. Jesus said a prayer and left the room. Peter, James, and John followed Him.

Jesus and His Apostles hurried through the streets of Jerusalem. The city was quiet. Peaceful. The city was asleep. Men were at rest, and the Son of God was about to begin His Way of the Cross.

When they reached the Garden of Olives, Jesus left the three Apostles near the garden wall. He asked them to watch while He went into the garden to pray.

The three men sat on the ground. It had been a long day, and the men were tired. They were soon fast asleep. But suddenly, Peter awoke with a start. There was a hand on his shoulder, the hand of his Master.

"Could you not watch one hour with me?" It was Jesus who asked the question.

Peter was ashamed. He made no excuse. He said nothing. The apostle knew that he had done wrong. He knew that he had hurt the Master.

Then Jesus left the men and went back into the garden to pray.

Soon there was a noise in the distance. Peter jumped to his feet. He could see lights — lights that were moving toward him. As the lights came closer, the noise became louder. Peter thought he heard voices. Yes, he did hear voices. Men's voices! Men were coming toward the Garden of Olives, and they were carrying lanterns.

Jesus, too, heard the noise, and He heard the voices. He hurried from the garden and stood by Peter's side. Four men stood in the darkness. Christ and His three apostles! Four silent men stood by the garden wall — wondering, waiting.

In a short time, a crowd of men stopped before Christ and His Apostles.

"Whom do you seek?" asked Jesus; He was very calm.

"Jesus of Nazareth!" called one of the men boldly.

Jesus was not surprised. He stepped forward and answered, "I am He."

Then a man stepped out of the crowd. It was Judas the apostle. Judas had led the men to the Garden of Olives. Judas had come to betray his Master.

"Hail, Master!" said Judas, and he kissed Christ.

That kiss was the signal. Several men rushed forward and caught hold of Christ. Jesus was at their mercy.

That was too much for Peter. Those men were not going to harm Christ, not if Peter could stop them. In a flash, Peter pulled out his sword and cut off the ear of one of the men.

But Jesus did not want Peter to fight. "Put up your sword!" He ordered. Then He touched the man's head and healed his wound.

Then the mob led Christ away. It was the beginning of the end.

Christ was gone. James and John had run away.

But not Peter! That night, Peter had promised Christ that he would not run away, and Peter meant to keep that promise. He followed the mob, but stayed at quite a distance from them.

The men took Jesus to the home of the high priest, Caiphas. While Christ was in the house, Peter managed to get into the courtyard. He walked through the crowd, but spoke to no one. There was a bonfire in the yard, and Peter stood near the fire to warm himself. Peter did not know it, but a girl was watching him.

The girl waited some minutes and then asked Peter a question: "You were with Jesus, were you not?"

The apostle tried to be calm. "I don't know what you are saying," he answered quickly and turned his head.

Peter had denied Christ. He denied Christ in order to save himself. He was ashamed, but he was afraid, too.

The apostle spent some unpleasant moments in that courtyard. He was afraid to leave, and he was afraid to stay. Then, once again, someone called Peter a disciple.

"I am not a disciple," he answered firmly.

Then the apostle became very bold. He began to talk to those about him. By doing this, he felt, people would not notice him. But one man did notice him.

"Did I not see you in the garden with Jesus?" asked the man as he pointed his finger.

Peter began to curse and swear. "I don't know Jesus," he answered sharply. "I don't know Him."

Just then Jesus was led through the courtyard. As He passed, Christ turned and looked at Peter, but He did not speak.

Then Peter remembered that Jesus had said that he would deny Him.

Peter rushed out of the courtyard into the night. He had denied his Master three times. He was a coward, a traitor. Christ's words had come true.

Chapter 11

Peter Learns a Lesson

It was Good Friday — the first Good Friday! A day of suffering for Christ! A day of misery for Peter! A day when Peter had plenty of time to think! His first thought, his great worry was whether Christ would forgive him. He had done wrong, and he was ashamed of himself. He was sorry from the bottom of his heart, and he wanted to tell Christ. But he could not do that. He was afraid that Christ's enemies would arrest him, so he took no chances. He remained in the house and tried to be patient.

About noon, a strange thing happened. The sun disappeared, and a cloud of darkness, which lasted for three hours, covered the earth. Those were three terrible hours for Peter. He knew that something was wrong. But the darkness! What did it mean?

That evening Peter left the house. He walked only a short distance when a stranger joined him.

"Were you at Calvary today?" began the stranger.

"Calvary! No, I was not."

The stranger stopped suddenly. He seemed to doubt Peter's words.

The stranger's surprise made Peter curious. "Why, what happened at Calvary?" asked the apostle.

The stranger's answer was a long one. The soldiers had tied Jesus to a post and beaten Him with whips. They had put a crown of long, sharp thorns on His head. His enemies then made Him carry a heavy Cross through the streets of Jerusalem. Jesus fell three times because the Cross was so heavy. Then the soldiers nailed Jesus to the Cross on the top of Mount Calvary. And for three long hours, while the world was in darkness, Jesus hung on the cross and suffered. Finally, He bowed His head and died.

Every word that the stranger spoke cut deep into Peter's heart. Jesus had been nailed to a Cross! The Master was dead! Cold sweat ran down the rough cheeks of the apostle. He shook from head to foot, and his heart pounded like a machine. Now he knew everything. Christ was dead. The Master was gone.

Peter thanked the stranger for his company and turned back. Peter wanted to be alone. He wanted to think.

Peter suffered that night and all the next day.

His heart was broken because he had lost his best Friend. What a terrible death for One who had been so kind! Peter knew that Jesus did not deserve that death. He could hardly believe that men could be so cruel.

Peter wondered about the future, and he worried about the apostles. Jesus had placed him in charge, and now that Jesus was gone, it was his duty to carry on the work of the Master. Peter knew what Jesus would want him to do, but he was afraid. He decided to wait.

The next morning, Mary of Magdala came to Peter and John and told them an exciting story. Mary had gone to visit Christ's tomb, and the grave was empty.

Christ's grave was empty!

Peter remembered that Christ had said that He would rise from the dead. The apostle's eyes almost jumped out of his head, and he wondered whether Mary had spoken the truth.

It was no time for questions. Mary led the way, and Peter and John followed her to the Master's tomb. Peter entered the tomb boldly. He found the white cloths that had been wrapped around the body of Christ, but the

body of Jesus was not there. The tomb was empty. Jesus Christ had risen from the dead.

Peter was so excited that he could not speak.

His heart jumped with joy. Never before had anyone risen from the dead. Christ had done the impossible. He had proved to the world that He was God. Now the world would have to believe.

Peter and John hurried back to the apostles to tell their story. There were questions, many questions, and the two apostles tried to answer all of them. But there were some questions that could not be answered: Where was the Master? Where had He gone?

All that day the Apostles remained together — wondering, watching, waiting.

That night, the door was locked, and suddenly Jesus stood in the center of the room. At first the Apostles were afraid. They could hardly believe their eyes.

"Peace to you! It is I. Do not be afraid!" Jesus said kindly.

Those words brought joy to the Apostles.

They were no longer afraid. There was peace in their souls.

Christ showed them the holes in His hands and His feet that the nails had made. He showed them His side that had been cut with a spear. He talked about His sufferings and death and answered questions. And to prove that He was really alive, Jesus ate some fish.

After He had eaten, Christ gave the Apostles a command and a promise. He ordered them to teach and to baptize all nations, and He promised to bless their work. Then Jesus gave the Apostles one of the greatest powers that has ever been given to men: the power to forgive sins — the power to hear confessions.

That was a happy moment for the Apostles. As priests, they now had the power to forgive sins, to cure the souls of men, to lead sinners back to Christ.

Jesus was very kind to Peter that night, and He never mentioned that the apostle had denied Him. Christ knew that Peter had made a mistake, and He knew that he was sorry.

That night, Peter learned a great lesson — a lesson that he never forgot. Jesus was kind to him, and forgave his great sin. From that moment Peter resolved to be kind to sinners, because he knew the joy of forgiveness.

Chapter 12

The First Pope

Jesus Christ has risen from the dead!" Those words were carried to every city, village, and town. For Christ's friends, it was a message of joy. For His enemies, it was a message of defeat. At first, many did not believe that Christ had risen from the dead, but later, when they saw Jesus, they had to believe.

Jesus spent forty days proving that He was really alive. He visited His friends, talked with people, and ate with them. He showed His wounds — the wounds in His hands, feet, and side. He even let people touch Him, because Christ wanted them to know that He was alive. He wanted all men to know He had risen from the dead.

Now, the Apostles were not with Jesus during all those forty days. They knew that they were going to begin their preaching soon, so they went to their homes for a last visit with their families and friends.

One evening, as Peter stood on the shore of the Lake of Galilee, he thought about the many times he had fished, and he longed to spend one more night on the lake he loved. He decided, therefore, to go fishing.

53

Peter invited some of the apostles, and they agreed to go with him. The men fished all night, but they caught nothing.

In the morning, when the apostles drew near the shore, they had a pleasant surprise. Jesus was there. He was sitting before a fire cooking some fish.

"Come and have breakfast with me!" called Christ as He raised His hand.

The apostles were overjoyed to hear the Master's voice. They hurried from the boat, waded through the water, and were soon on land. They were a happy group, as they ate their morning meal on the shore of the lake.

After breakfast, Jesus asked His leader a question: "Peter, do you love me?"

That question took Peter by surprise. But Peter was not lost for an answer.

"Yes, Lord, You know that I love You."

Jesus nodded His head and answered with three words: "Feed my lambs."

Then a second time Jesus asked the same question, and Peter gave the same answer. Again, Christ ordered Peter to feed His lambs.

Finally, for the third time, Jesus asked, "Peter, do you love me?"

Peter was disturbed. "Lord," he answered, "You know all things. You know that I love You."

Then Christ gave the same order again: "Feed my sheep."

"Feed my lambs. Feed my sheep." Those words made Peter the Shepherd of Christ's Church. Like a shepherd, Peter was to watch over and protect the Church. He was to lead and guide those who believed in Christ. He was to have all of Christ's powers. He was to take Christ's place.

"Feed my lambs. Feed my sheep." Those six words made Peter the head of Christ's Church. Those six words made Peter the first Pope.

Chapter 13

The First Miracle

Christ's work was done. He had founded His Church, and it was time for Him to go back to His Father. So, forty days after He arose from the dead, Jesus raised Himself from the ground and ascended into Heaven. Never again on the earth did the Apostles hear the Master's voice. Never again did they walk with Jesus in Galilee. Never again did they see His mighty miracles. The joys and pleasures of three long years were at an end. Jesus was gone. The Apostles were left behind.

The Apostles were to teach all nations, and they were anxious to begin their work. They wanted to teach and preach. But the last thing that Jesus told them was that they should stay in Jerusalem until they received help from Heaven. Help from Heaven! Those were words that the Apostles did not understand.

The Apostles obeyed Christ and remained in Jerusalem. They locked themselves in a room with Mary, the Mother of Jesus. They were afraid of the Jews, and they spent their time in prayer. On the tenth day, as they were praying, they heard a loud noise, a noise that sounded like a mighty wind. The Apostles and Mary stopped their prayers and looked at one another, but no one spoke. They were afraid, and they wondered!

Suddenly, the room became very bright. Pieces of fire floated through the air in the upper part of the room. Then the fire came down slowly and stopped over the heads of each of the Apostles. Those pieces of fire, you know, were the Holy Spirit coming to the Apostles. Each of the Apostles received the Holy Spirit.

Did the Holy Spirit change the Apostles? Yes! After they had received the Holy Spirit, the Apostles became strong and brave. They were no longer afraid of the Jews. They were ready to preach for Christ. The Holy Spirit was help from Heaven — the help that Christ had promised them.

The coming of the Holy Spirit meant a great deal to Peter. He knew that, even though Jesus was gone, the Master had not forgotten His Apostles. He knew, too, that the Apostles were anxious to begin their work. He was their leader, and he decided to show them what they were expected to do. That very day, Peter led the other apostles into the streets of Jerusalem, and he preached his first sermon.

A large crowd gathered to hear the new preacher, and they were surprised that Peter spoke with such power. Why, this was the fisherman from Galilee! A rough, simple man, with no education! How was it that he spoke so easily? And what did Peter say? Did Peter have a new

message for the Jews? No! He spoke about Christ: His work, His miracles, His death, His coming back to life. He begged the Jews to do penance, to be baptized, to believe in Christ. Peter's words were simple, but they came from his heart.

When Peter finished, three thousand Jews begged to be baptized. Three thousand Jews came into Christ's Church.

Peter was happy. His first sermon won three thousand souls for Christ. It was a fine start, a grand beginning. The fisherman from Galilee was beginning to catch men.

About three o'clock in the afternoon, Peter and the apostle John went up to the temple to pray. At the gate of the temple sat a lame beggar. This man had never walked in all the forty years of his life. As Peter and John passed through the gate, the lame man begged for money.

Peter's heart was touched. He felt very sorry for the beggar, and he wanted to help him. Peter stopped, looked at the beggar, and nodded his head.

"I have no silver or gold," said Peter to the lame man, "but what I have, I give you. In the name of Jesus Christ of Nazareth, arise and walk!"

Peter took the lame man by the hand and helped him to his feet. Then the man began to walk. Peter had cured him. The apostle had worked a miracle. His first miracle in the name of Jesus Christ!

The beggar was so happy that he jumped with joy. It was the first time in his life that he had ever walked, and his first thought was to give thanks. So, Peter, John, and the beggar walked into the temple.

Three men knelt in the temple in prayer.

A beggar! An apostle! The first Pope! Three grateful hearts gave thanks to God.

Chapter 14

Peter Dares His Enemies

Peter's miracle caused great excitement in the city of Jerusalem. While many were pleased, the enemies of Christ received the news with hatred in their hearts. They felt that Christ's death was the end of His Church, the end of His followers. But Peter's miracle proved that they were wrong.

"We must stop Peter," cried the enemies of the Church. "We must stop him, because he will cause trouble."

Those wicked men lost no time in carrying out their threat. They arrested Peter and put him in prison.

The next day, Peter was placed on trial. But what had he done? He had done no wrong. He had been kind to a beggar. He had cured a man who was lame. Could Peter be punished for being kind? Hardly!

Peter was allowed to go free, but his enemies warned him that he would have to stop his preaching. He was not to teach in the name of Jesus Christ.

Peter said nothing. He knew that Jesus had ordered him to teach. He was not afraid of men. He was not afraid of their threats.

Peter was no coward. He left the prison and at once began to preach again. Great crowds followed him wherever he went, and many came from nearby cities to hear the great apostle. The sick and lame were carried to him, and Peter cured every one of them. The people knew that Peter had power, and they knew that his power came from Christ. Hundreds of people followed the apostle and became members of the Church of Christ.

The Church was growing. That was bad news for Peter's enemies, so they arrested the apostle again and put him in prison. This time Peter was worried. He knew only too well what the Jews had done to Christ. He wondered what the Jews would do to him. Perhaps he would have to suffer, too. As he sat in his prison cell, some terrible thoughts passed through the apostle's mind, but there was nothing he could do. He could only wait — and hope and pray.

Peter's prayers were answered that night, and they were answered in a strange way. The prison cell was a dark place, but suddenly the room became very bright. Peter saw an angel standing near the door. The angel opened the door of the cell and told Peter to follow him. The apostle walked quickly and was soon in the prison yard. He was free again. No one had seen the angel. No one had seen the apostle leave the prison cell. Peter thanked the angel for his help, and then the angel disappeared.

The next morning, Peter dared to go into the temple. He even dared to preach, but the prison guards soon

found him. He was brought back to prison and placed on trial.

"We ordered you not to teach," spoke one of the officers roughly, "and you have disobeyed."

Peter was brave. "I must obey God rather than men," answered the apostle. Peter's answer came as a surprise. The soldiers and guards hated this man who dared to defy them.

"Let us put him to death!" they called out in anger.

But one of the chief officers quieted the angry men. He ordered the guards to take Peter into another room. Then the chief officer spoke to the soldiers.

"Men of Israel," he warned them, "be careful what you do! Leave Peter alone! If Peter is working for God, then you are fighting God. If you fight God, you cannot win. If you fight God, you must lose."

The soldiers agreed that the chief officer was right, but they felt that Peter should be punished. They decided, therefore, that Peter should be whipped. So, the soldiers stripped the prisoner to the waist and tied his hands to a stone. Then the men struck Peter with pieces of leather — thirteen times on his chest, thirteen times on his right shoulder, and thirteen times on his left. Thirty-nine blows! Thirty-nine blows that caused great pain to the apostle, but he suffered them all in silence. As each blow struck, Peter thought about Christ. Jesus, too, had been whipped, and now he was suffering in the same way — suffering for his Master.

After the whipping, Peter was set free. But the soldiers warned the apostle that he was not to teach in the name of Jesus Christ.

Peter listened, but made no promises. He left the prison, and every day Peter went to the temple. Every day he went from house to house. Every day the apostle preached and taught in the name of Jesus Christ.

Chapter 15

The Wicked King

G o into the whole world, and preach the gospel to every
creature!" Those were the words of Jesus Christ.
That was the order that Jesus had given to the Apostles.
Jesus wanted them to teach not only the people of Jerusalem, or the people of Judea and Galilee. He wanted them
to teach the whole world.

Peter and the other apostles worked hard to carry out
this order of the Master. They went into cities, villages,
and towns and preached the words of Christ. They traveled far and wide and worked long hours. Nothing was
too hard for them as they tried to bring souls to Christ.

Wherever they went, the Apostles started churches,
and they placed men in charge of those churches. Those
men were called "disciples" or "helpers of the Apostles."
Those disciples taught the same things that the Apostles
taught, and they cared for the new members of the Church.
In this way, the Church became strong, and the Apostles
were able to go to new places and make new beginnings.

Those were the first days of the Church of Christ.
They were the first years of the Catholic Church. The

beginnings were small, but the Church grew. The work was not easy, because the enemies of the Church made it hard for the Apostles and their disciples.

During those first years, Peter spent his time visiting the churches — preaching, teaching, and helping the disciples. He visited the people, too, and cured their sick. Wherever he went, Peter was greeted as head of the Church. He was in charge of all churches, and the people looked to him to lead and guide them.

At first the city of Jerusalem was the center of the Catholic Church. But Jerusalem was out of the way, and it was hard to reach that city. So, in the year 40, when the Church was seven years old, Peter moved the center, or the Mother Church, to the city of Antioch. Two years later, the city of Rome became the center of the Catholic Church.

At this time, Herod Agrippa was king of the Jewish people. Herod was liked by the Jews, but he was a jealous man. He was jealous of the Catholic Church. Herod felt that the Church was becoming too strong. Too many people were leaving the Jewish religion and becoming followers of the apostle. How could Herod stop them? That was the question that bothered the jealous king.

Herod schemed and planned for a long time. Then he decided to act. He decided to punish the leaders of the Church. This cruel king felt that if he destroyed the leaders, then the Church would be destroyed. A Church without leaders would soon die. That was the way Herod argued with himself, and that was his plan: to destroy the leaders of the Catholic Church.

It was time for the feast of the Pasch, the great feast day of the Jewish people. Jews from every land left their homes and went to Jerusalem. Peter, too, went to Jerusalem to celebrate the feast.

Herod heard that Peter was in Jerusalem. "Peter is here," smiled the cruel king to himself. "This is my chance to catch a big fish."

King Herod lost no time in carrying out his wicked plan. He had Peter arrested and thrown into prison. Peter was marked for death.

Peter knew that his time had finally come. There was no chance for him to escape. How could he escape when he was chained to the prison floor? How could he escape when four soldiers guarded him day and night? It was a sad ending, but Peter did not complain. He prayed a great deal, and prayer gave him strength. Prayer made him brave, and he wanted to die a brave man.

Peter did not have to spend many days in prison, but they were hard days. Peter's cell was damp and cold and dark. He worried about what was happening to the other apostles and to his people. Each morning the apostle wondered whether that day would be his last. When evening came, he wondered again: Shall I die tomorrow? Where shall I die? How shall I die?

One night, while Peter slept, he was suddenly awakened. Someone struck him on the side. It was an angel.

"Come quickly!" whispered the angel. "Follow me."

Peter jumped to his feet, and the chains fell from his hands. He followed the angel swiftly through the prison gate and down a dark street. Then, suddenly, Peter found that he was alone. The angel had disappeared. The angel was gone. Peter was free.

"Where is Peter?" That was the cry of the soldiers when they found the empty cell. The next morning that was also the cry of the angry Herod. "Where is Peter? Where did he go?" But that was Peter's secret.

Herod Agrippa ordered his soldiers to search the city and find the apostle. The soldiers searched everywhere, but they returned without Peter.

Herod flew into a rage, but his anger did not harm the apostle. A wicked king had lost his fight against God.

Chapter 16

Rome

G od takes care of His friends, and He never allows His
work to suffer. In the year 44, Almighty God took
care of the early Christians, because in that year, King
Herod died. He died as he lived — a most cruel death.

Herod's death brought peace to the Church. No longer did the Christians have to suffer. They taught and
practiced their religion without fear. It was a pleasant
change, and the work of the Church — the work of
Christ — went forward.

After his escape from prison, Peter went up north to
the city of Antioch and traveled through the countries of
Asia. Now and then he returned to Jerusalem to help the
disciples in their great work. Whenever he spoke, Peter's
message was always the same. He talked about Christ —
what Jesus said and did. He told about Christ's miracles
and how those miracles proved that Christ was God.
Then Peter urged the people to follow Christ.

On those journeys, Peter baptized, and he started many
new churches. Christ was his Partner, and together, Christ
and Peter caught many fish.

The Man Who Never Died

While Peter was pleased with the way the Church was growing, still he was not fully satisfied. Perhaps he was impatient. Perhaps he expected too much in a short time. But the apostle was anxious to have the whole world know Christ's message, and he wanted the whole world to have that message as soon as possible.

Peter had his eyes on Rome. The great city of Rome! The city of wealth, the city of sin! Peter had heard terrible stories about Rome. He had heard about the sins of the people who lived there. The people of Rome needed Christ. They needed Christ's message, and Peter knew it.

Rome! He must go to Rome. That was what Peter decided. So for several days, Peter sailed the Mediterranean Sea. Finally he reached the city of Rome. He was a stranger in a strange city. And little did the people of that city know what Peter was bringing to them.

Those first days in Rome were sad days for the apostle. He found that the stories he had heard were true. Rome was a wicked city. It was a city of sin. The rich people held all the power, and they spent their time feasting, eating, and drinking. They believed that death was the end of everything, and they did not believe in God.

Every rich family had hundreds of slaves. These slaves worked hard, and were treated like animals. The life of a slave was a life of work, a life without happiness.

Now, there were many Jews in Rome, but they lived in a separate part of the city. The Romans looked down upon the Jews. They hated them. The Jews really lived in a separate world. They had their houses of prayer, and they kept the Jewish feasts. They fasted, prayed, and were good people. Most of them were poor, but their hearts were right.

At first Peter could hardly believe what he saw. He was shocked, horrified. He wondered how the Romans would receive him. Would they listen to his message? Would the Roman people accept Christ?

Peter's heart was heavy. He knew that there were hard days ahead of him, but he knew, too, that God was on his side. He was determined to give his best to the people of Rome because they needed God so much.

Peter's first days were spent with the Jews in their part of the city. He lived with them, made friends with them, and prayed in their churches. He did not teach, nor did he preach, and he told no one why he was in Rome. No one knew that Peter was the great apostle. The people thought that he was just another Jew.

Peter began his work by talking about Christ to a few of his new friends. Then he spoke to more people, and these people told their friends. After a while, groups of people met in homes and listened to the apostle. It was a small beginning, but it was a good beginning, because many of the people begged to be baptized. As the months passed, the number of Christians grew, and before long they had their own church.

Peter was happy. His work was beginning to bear fruit. He had one church in the great city of Rome. He had founded the Church of Christ there, and down through the years the eyes of the world were to look upon that Church as the center of truth. That Church was to be the center of the world.

But Peter's work was not finished. There were still thousands and thousands of people in Rome who had not heard about Christ, and Peter was determined to reach all of them. He was not satisfied with a few. He wanted all Rome for Christ. After all, Christ's message was not for a few Jews: it was for all Jews and for those who were not Jews. It was for the slaves and for their masters. It was for the poor and for the rich. Even those who prayed to the statues of stone must be told about Christ. One church in Rome was not enough to take care of all the people. That one church was only a beginning, the beginning of Peter's dream — a dream that, one day, Rome would be a city of churches, and those churches would hold on high the Cross of Jesus Christ.

Peter never seemed to get tired. He loved his work, and he never complained. Patient, kind, filled with love of his Master, he was a real apostle. His work in Rome brought thousands of Jews to Christ. He saw his numbers grow. He saw new churches rise. He saw men, women, and children leave the Jewish churches and walk in the footsteps of the great Master.

After working many months with the Jews in Rome, Peter gave his attention to the slaves. First, he taught them that all men are equal. That was good news for the slaves. Then he told them how Jesus loved the poor, how the poor had first place in the heart of Christ. That was enough to make the slaves want to hear more about Christ. No wonder they listened to Peter's words! No wonder they begged to be baptized!

Peter also spoke to the shopkeepers, the servants, the common people, the soldiers, and the rich. Some of them shook their heads and refused to believe. Others, thousands of others, became members of Christ's Church.

For twenty years Peter worked in the city of Rome. It was hard work, but it was happy work, too. During all that time, no one found fault and no one disturbed the work of the apostle. Even the young emperor, Nero, did not complain. While Nero was not a religious man, still he allowed his people to go to church wherever they wished. And so, the Church of Rome grew and became strong.

Peter was now an old man. He was past sixty.

His shoulders were bent, and his beard was white. An old man who had spent the best years of his life working for Christ!

But Peter had no regrets. He had baptized thousands. He had built churches. He had ordained priests. Peter had brought Christ to the city of Rome.

Chapter 17

The Arrest

One night in July, in the year 64, the cry of "Fire!" rang through the city of Rome. The city was on fire.

For nine days the city burned. Churches, homes, and public buildings were destroyed, and hundreds of people lost their lives. They were nine days of agony, suffering, and death. Never before had the Romans suffered so much. More than half of their city was destroyed. It was the greatest blow that had ever struck the proud city.

What caused that terrible fire? That was the question that the Roman people asked. Many of them thought they knew the answer. They blamed the twenty-seven-year-old emperor, Nero. Many times Nero had said that he wanted a new city, a more beautiful city, a city with buildings made of gold and silver and precious stones. The people remembered what Nero had said, and they felt quite sure that he had burned the city in order to have his wish.

Then, too, the people heard that, during the fire, Nero was very happy — so happy that he had sung songs.

That story made the people angry: it filled them with hatred. Many said that they would make Nero suffer, and some even wished to kill him.

When Nero heard that the people were angry, he was afraid. "These people may take my life," he said to himself. "Something must be done to stop them."

The emperor knew that he would have to act quickly. He wondered how he could change the angry people. Whom could he blame for the burning of Rome?

A wicked thought flashed through the emperor's mind. He decided he would blame the Christians and punish them, too. In this way he felt he would save and protect himself.

Nero lost no time in carrying out his sinful plan.

He arrested hundreds of Christians and threw them into prison. But that was only the beginning. Nero even planned how to make those Christians suffer. Some of them were wrapped in the skins of wild animals and were left to be eaten by dogs. Others, fastened to crosses, died like their Master. Others were burned alive. Many were covered with tar and set on fire, to serve as torches during the night in the gardens of Nero.

Those were dark, bitter days for the Christians of Rome. Any person who said that he believed in Christ was put to death. They were hard days for the Church, but the Christians remained faithful. They met and prayed in secret, and no madman, no cruel emperor was able to take away their love for Christ.

For months, Nero made the Christians suffer. He even made shows at night so that the people could watch the Christians die. It seemed as though there was no end to his cruelty and madness.

But where was Peter? Where was Peter during those days of terrible suffering?

The apostle was in Rome. At first, he hid himself, and some of his friends wanted him to leave the city. But Peter would not run away. He was no coward, and he was not afraid to die. He knew that the Church needed him. He knew that the Christians needed him, and, like a good shepherd, he stayed with his sheep. Peter spent his time visiting the Christians in secret — praying with them, urging them to be brave, and preparing their souls for God.

For some time, Peter managed to escape the cruelty of Nero, but the great apostle was not forgotten. Nero knew that Peter, the leader of the Christians, would be a great prize. But the emperor decided to take his time and save his prize for a special occasion.

Finally, after many months, Nero ordered his soldiers to find the apostle. They were to search the city, and they were not to return without Peter.

The soldiers obeyed the emperor's orders. They went first to the Jewish part of the city because they thought Peter would be hiding there. But Peter was not hiding. He was visiting with friends when suddenly the door opened, and four soldiers entered the room.

"Are you Peter, the leader of the Christians?" asked one of the soldiers.

"I am," answered Peter gently. "What do you wish?"

"We have orders from the emperor to arrest you."

Peter knew that his time had come. He knew that it would do no good to argue and that he could not escape. Peter was very calm and offered to go with the soldiers without causing trouble.

The soldiers led Peter through the streets of Rome. The Rome that Peter had learned to love! The Rome where he had spent over twenty years of his life! Was this the last time he would walk these streets? Peter felt that he knew the answer.

The soldiers put Peter in prison, and his hands and feet were bound with chains. By order of the emperor, the apostle was guarded every minute of the day and night. Nero was determined that Peter would not escape.

The Pope of Rome was a prisoner. And why was the Pope a prisoner? Peter was a prisoner because he had walked in the footsteps of Jesus Christ. And, like his Master, Peter was beginning to carry his cross.

Chapter 18

The Cross

A prison is not a cheerful place, nor is a prison cell. The cell where Peter was held was underground. It was dark, dreary, damp, cold. It was no place for a sixty-six-year-old man. But Peter did not complain. He was patient and suffered in silence.

Peter's greatest suffering came from his chains. They were heavy and were fastened tightly. They were so short that he was not able to walk about the cell. At night, the chains disturbed his sleep. Since he was able to get little sleep, most of his nights were spent in prayer.

During all his days in prison, Peter's only companions were his guards. Although the soldiers talked with him, still, they were not very friendly. They were afraid to be too friendly, because someone might think they were Christians.

Days and weeks passed. They were long days, and longer nights. Days and nights of pain, suffering, waiting, and wondering! Every day was the same, and the nights were no different. The prisoner was weak and nervous. He longed for the day when his sufferings would end.

The Man Who Never Died

One evening, while Peter sat in his cell, he heard a
strange noise. It was the sound of marching feet. Then a
voice called through the darkness.

The door of Peter's cell opened, and nine soldiers entered the room. Eight of the men carried swords. Their
leader held a lantern.

One of the soldiers took the lantern and held it
above his head. The leader unrolled a paper and began to
read:

"Rome has no place, and no mercy, for enemies. For
twenty-five years, Peter, you have been an enemy. You
have placed Christ before the emperor, and by your
preaching, you have disturbed the peace of this city.
Therefore, by order of the emperor, you shall die tomorrow, the twenty-ninth day of June, the year 67, the thir-
teenth year of the reign of Nero. You shall be nailed to a
cross before the crowds of Rome, and may your death be
a warning to others!"

Peter tried to be calm. He tried to be brave. But his
heart pounded within him. Cold sweat poured from his
forehead.

For a moment he was cold and weak, but suddenly, he
thought about Christ on His Cross. That thought gave
Peter courage and strength. Standing erect, the apostle
began to speak.

"I find no fault with the sentence of the emperor.
Death to me means the beginning of a new life — a new
life with Jesus Christ. I have only one favor to ask of you.

I am not worthy to die like my Master. Therefore, when you nail me to the cross, place my head downward!"

No other words were spoken. The soldiers left in silence, and Peter remained in his prison cell.

That night the apostle did not even try to sleep. Every minute, every second was precious — too precious to spend in sleeping. Every moment of that night was spent with God — thanking God for His blessings, begging God to give him strength and courage to die well.

The next day was a holiday for the city of Rome. Thousands of people crowded into the Circus of Nero to watch a man die. A fisherman from Galilee! The Pope of Rome!

When Peter was led into the Circus, there was an uproar. The crowd stood and cheered and clapped their hands. Those wicked people knew that the Pope of Rome would soon be dead.

Peter was a sad picture. He was so weak from his stay in prison that he found it hard to walk, but he managed to walk without help.

At first the crowd startled him. He stopped for a moment, then he bowed his head. As Peter walked to the center of the great theater, he prayed for his enemies and for Nero. He begged God to forgive them.

In the center of the Circus, Peter was nailed to a cross. Then the cross was raised that all might see. At last, Nero had his wish. But Peter had his wish, too. He was nailed to the cross with his head downward.

Peter did not suffer long. He was too weak to suffer much. In a short time, one of the soldiers raised his sword. That was the signal. Peter, the apostle, was dead — that was what the world thought. But the world was wrong. . . .

Chapter 19

The Man Who Never Died

When Peter hung with his head downward, he must have smiled. Here is the reason: today in the city of Rome, almost on the same spot where Peter hung on the cross, stands the world's greatest church. The church of St. Peter!

Next to the church of St. Peter is a large building called the Vatican. In the Vatican lives the Pope. The world calls the Pope "Peter." We call the Pope "Peter" because the man in the Vatican is the man who takes Peter's place.

The man on the cross died, but Peter did not die. The man in the Vatican dies, but the Pope always lives.

Now you know why Peter smiled when he hung with his head downward. He knew that the Church would always have another Pope to take his place. He knew there would always be a Peter. He knew there would always be a Pope.

Now you know why Peter was the man who never died.

About the Author

Gerald Thomas Brennan was born in 1898 in Rochester, New York, where he attended St. Andrew's and St. Bernard's seminaries and was ordained in 1923. He served as pastor of Rochester's Mount Carmel Church and later of St. Bridget's. He taught in the parish schools and preached special homilies for young people during the weekly children's Mass at his parishes. These homilies were so popular that a friend urged Fr. Brennan to have them published.

Fr. Brennan's numerous children's books, including Angel City, The Ghost of Kingdom Come, The Man Who Dared a King, and The Good Bad Boy, have been enjoyed by children all over the world.

Fr. Brennan died in 1962.

Sophia Institute Press®

Sophia Institute® is a nonprofit institution that seeks to restore man's knowledge of eternal truth, including man's knowledge of his own nature, his relation to other persons, and his relation to God. Sophia Institute Press® serves this end in numerous ways: it publishes translations of foreign works to make them accessible to English-speaking readers; it brings out-of-print books back into print; and it publishes important new books that fulfill the ideals of Sophia Institute®. These books afford readers a rich source of the enduring wisdom of mankind.

Sophia Institute Press® makes these high-quality books available to the general public by using advanced technology and by soliciting donations to subsidize its publishing costs. Your generosity can help Sophia Institute Press® to provide the public with editions of works containing the enduring wisdom of the ages. Please send your tax-deductible contribution to the address below.

For your free catalog,
Call toll-free: 1-800-888-9344

Sophia Institute Press® • Box 5284 • Manchester, NH 03108
www.sophiainstitute.com

Sophia Institute® is a tax-exempt institution as defined by the Internal Revenue Code, Section 501(c)(3). Tax I.D. 22-2548708.